Heartfelt Expressions

A Book of Inspirational and Enlightening Poetry

Carol A. Ennis

Heartfelt Expressions

ISBN 978-0-9848641-4-0
Library of Congress Control Number: 2012910648

Genre: Poetry/Inspirational
Publisher: Angel Wings Publications, LLC
Email: angelwingspub@yahoo.com
Website: www.angelwingspublications.com

Book Cover Design: Donna Osborn Clark at CreationByDonna.com

Cover Photo: George W. Baldi, III

Editor: Donna Osborn Clark

Typeset & Interior Design: www.CreationByDonna.com

Angel Wings Publications, LLC
P.O. Box 96
Vauxhall, NJ 07088

This book is dedicated in the loving memory of:
My beloved mother – Anna L. Malone
1923-2011

"Mom I will meet you in paradise."

Acknowledgments

In life we have dreams, and in order to make our dreams come true, we must be willing to take that step forward, and promise ourselves that there will be no turning back. We must be of great courage, and not lose sight of our dream, knowing that we can make it happen. It gives us encouragement to know that there are true friends and family who will be there to pick you up when you fall.

I want to take this opportunity to first of all thank God for His grace and His mercy in which He has bestowed upon me.

I want to thank Sharon Wells and Donna Osborn Clark who inspired me not to give up, and for sharing their knowledge and expertise in book writing.

I want to give special thanks to my Editor Donna Osborn Clark for her professional experience and her beautiful works of art in designing my book cover, her creations and for adding that special touch to my poetry.

Introduction

It's what's inside the heart that makes a difference in some one's life.
"Believing in yourself is an important aspect in life.
If you believe in yourself, and put your mind into what
it is that you want to do, you can do anything."
Carol A. Ennis

Reading is a part of life and living. Without reading, how will we learn? Reading helps us expand our minds. It assists us in making the best choices for our lives based on what we have read and learned from it along with parental guidance. It gives us a sense of hope in becoming a part of something in life. In order to be successful in life, you must believe that all things are possible. You must set a goal, and work hard to achieve it. Sometimes all it takes is someone to believe in you, and tell you everything is going to be alright. The most important thing is to love what you do.

At an early age, before I became a teenager, it seems as though poetry evolved around my whole life. I remember each day at school, when the school bell rang, I would go dashing out of the school yard with excitement. I could not wait to get home so I could write down all the thoughts that were going through my head. Naturally I was excited. When all of the other kids were out to play, I would lock my bedroom door; pull out a piece of paper from my notebook, and start writing poetry. Dinner was an important time back then, especially when my parents were struggling to keep food on the table. But I didn't care much about that, my hunger was for poetry. Anytime you would rather write poetry than eat, you had to be excited.

By my developing such a passion for writing, in my junior high school years, I signed up for Creative Writing as one of my subjects. I would get A's on my report card. Throughout my entire school years, onto high school, Creative Writing was my favorite subject, and I was always writing poems.

I remember one day I saw an advertisement in the newspaper about a poetry contest. Anyone who wanted to enter the contest had to send in an original poem of their own, and you were only allowed so many words. There was a deadline, and if you should win, you would be notified and you would receive your prize in the mail.

There were first, second and third place prizes. To my surprise, a letter came in the mail with a check enclosed. I had won. I remember running down the stairs with so much anticipation. I showed my mother the letter, and a big smile came over her face. She said: "Aw that is so nice." She said you got talent child. Somehow along the way, the letter was lost after our family moved. I wanted to frame it as a reminder that I can do anything if I put my mind to it, and that I can succeed. All was not lost, that was my beginning to a never ending journey to what I love most, poetry.

Every year for my mom and dad's anniversary, I would prepare a skit, and I would write a poem to them. I was the chosen one to read all the anniversary cards. When it came time for me to read my poem, everybody would gather around the table, my mom and dad sitting there waiting patiently as all got quiet. Mom would always close her eyes when I read the poem so that she could absorb every word. Afterwards, everybody would applaud me. Then I would embrace my mom with a big hug and a kiss, and she would thank me and tell me how beautiful the poem was and how much she loved me. She said my poems always touched her heart, and that it meant so much to her and my dad. Then she would go on to say that I missed my calling.

The feeling that came over me when I read my poetry was over whelming. We had such a strong bond between family, and family is everything to me. It is all about putting love into all that you do that makes it so unique and special. Being able to express the love you feel for family without saying the words.

When I write poems for someone, I am able to connect to that person, and I can feel the energy, whether it is joy or sorrow. It is a God sent gift to be able to connect with someone through my writing. I could be most anywhere, and when a poem or words come to mind, I want to be able to write them down. I thank God for giving me the gift of writing, and I pray that my book will touch many hearts and minds, and that whatever your gift, use it to the Glory of God and you will succeed.

Table of Contents

BELIEVING

Carol A. Ennis

Branch Out

Let not your heart be troubled
Even when things make you sad
Explore the possibilities in your life
The excitement should make you glad.

Life has so much to offer you
Even when the sun doesn't shine
You really owe it to yourself
It is time to make up your mind.

There will always be someone to cheer you on
Someone to encourage you
To help you get back on track again
Make life more enjoyable too.
Toss out all of the old things
Add meaning to the life you choose
Branch out and take that step forward
What do you have to lose?

Believe In Yourself

Believe in yourself my troubled friend
Because someone believes in you
When the troubles never seem to cease
You just don't know what to do.

Believe in yourself when the chips are down
When your friends turn their backs on you
Believe in yourself with all your heart
It is totally up to you.

Eliminate all the negative thinking
Leave the unpleasant experiences behind
Believe in yourself and don't dwell on the pass
Then peace you will be able to find.

Don't let life's burdens get you down
There isn't a minute to waste
Take it step by step one day at a time
Then you can slowly pick up the pace.

If you want to accomplish your goals in life
Focus on what is important to you
Let that positive energy flow through your mind
You will accomplish all you set out to do.

Carol A. Ennis

Broken Pieces

Pick up the broken pieces
The bad memories it is time to erase
Start putting your life back together
All the shattered pieces back in place.
Open the door to a new future
Let nothing shut you out
You must believe that it can happen
In your mind there should be no doubt.

If you fail to connect the pieces
Don't give up just try again
If you get discouraged along the way
Remember it is a far cry from where you have been.

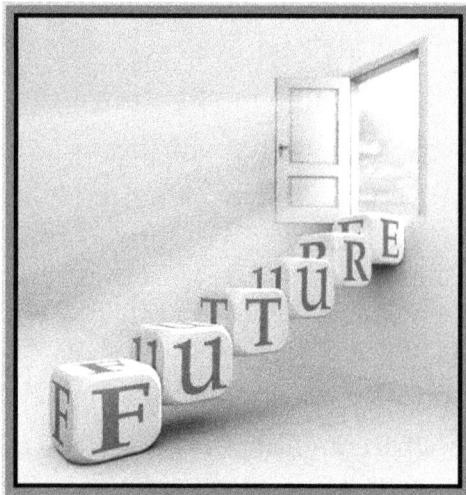

Faith's Journey

Oh holy and everlasting spirit
Yes, I am still alive
Because of my faith and your presence
Is the only way I could have survived.

I speak not of these words in silence
Of the mental and emotional pain
But of how God showed me mercy
When He washed away the stain.

I ask where would I be today
If it wasn't for God's love and His grace
Through all of my pain and suffering
I continued to seek His face.

In Him I have found peace and comfort
He never left me alone
He picked me up when I stumbled
He carried me all the way home.

With God I have become a survivor
I can now see through His eyes
Each morning when I wake up
I know it was He who helped me rise.

Carol A. Ennis

Follow Your Dream

Spread your wings and reach for the stars
Toss those unpleasant memories into the sea
Set your goals and follow your dreams
Be the best that you can be.

Time is of great essence
Don't let it slip away
If you don't make it happen
There is no promise of another day.

Hold on when you feel life is shutting you out
Have faith each and every day
Know that you are special in this life
You will always find a way.

Heartfelt Expressions

Never Give Up

Sometimes things happen in your life
You feel it just isn't fair
The burdens you carry that weigh you down
It makes life so hard to bear.
Faith will give you strength to recover
Remember the promise that was made to you
Along with those precious memories of the past
Of all the things you use to do.

Whenever you are feeling down and out
You feel that you need a friend
Just reach out to those who love you
They will support you to the end.
The light in your life may seem dim right now
You're having a hard time finding your way
No matter what the problem is
There will always be a brighter day.

Carol A. Ennis

The Storm Is Almost Gone

It seems as though every time you look around
There is pain and suffering everywhere
At times we often wonder, how much more can we bear.
All the things that have happened, all that we have been through
All the things that we had planned for, we never had a chance to do.

We felt like we were shipwrecked in a cold and stormy sea
Trying to reach the dry lands, too much fog we could not see.
Once the storm is over, and we are shipped to shore
We put away our umbrellas, and again it begins to poor.
Even when the sun is out, the storm is still yet to come.
There is one storm after another, where are they coming from?

Those precious peaceful moments, they seem to disappear
Then one trial after another, we can't seem to think very clear.
There is always a lesson to be learned, we must accept what we cannot change
It is not an easy thing to do, because it is our lives we must re-arrange.

Whatever is meant to come to pass, no matter how great the pain
We don't quite know the reason, but we know there is much to gain.
We must always keep an open mind, focus on the blessings we receive everyday
Believing the storm will soon be over, and there will be a brighter day.

There Is Hope

There is always hope for tomorrow
Through all the pain and sorrow.
From the fear, the helplessness, the guilt and shame
The anger, sadness, the flashbacks the pain.
Depression, anxiety, the low self-esteem
The cold sweats, the sleepless nights, even the bad dreams.

My mind is in a turmoil trying to find a safe place to hide
Each day is filled with guilt, so many nights I have cried.
Without having a life raft, I drifted too far out to sea
I called out for someone to help me, someone to rescue me.

The darkness had overshadowed me; there was no one else in sight
I raised my eyes and looked upward, it was then I saw the light.
At that very moment, one of Heaven's Angels had appeared
As the darkness had been lifted, my mind became very clear.
I seemed to have regained my confidence, a desire to start a new
The hope of change to overcome all that I have been through.

Hope became my boldness, after all the suffering and pain
Realizing even with new found joy and peace
My life will never be the same.
I promised to keep the hope alive, each and every day
When God sent down His Angel
I knew it was He who paved the way.

Carol A. Ennis

Hardships

We know at times the road gets rough
The hardships we have to face
We must learn to take one step at a time
While learning how to slow down our pace.
It is difficult to walk through that unknown place
More difficult to walk it alone
Having the love and support of family
Knowing you can pick up the telephone.

All the doubts and fears we have, is merely just a test
The only thing that we can do is to give our very best.
We all at times have been weakened
By trials and tribulations to great lengths
That is why family comes together
To build up each other's strength.
Even though there will be darkness
There is still that burning light
Let us put our arms around each other
Never give up the fight.

Have much patience to hold out
To see what the end is going to be
Remember faith is the key to much happiness
Your day will soon come you will see.
There are times when we feel so down and out,
It is hard to make it through day to day

Even find ourselves confused, but we must never lose our way.
There are always answers, to all the questions we may ask
That is why one day all our suffering,
Will become a thing of the past.
We should always be there for one another,
Every step of the way
Learn to bear each other's burdens,
Knowing family is here to stay.

A Wish

It doesn't matter who you are
To make a dream come true
When this blessing is bestowed upon your heart
This wish is just for you.

You have the power to change things
The opportunity will come your way
You must connect with your inner spirit
Your wish will be granted one day.

Carol A. Ennis

Life

In life we can accept things we cannot change
Or let life just pass us by
Especially when faced with difficult times
You must have faith and give life another try.
When life holds so many burdens for us
We tend to find someone else to blame
If we could reach deep down within ourselves
Our lives would surely change.

The mind is such a delicate thing
It is so easy to get off track
Before we know it we have lost so much time
It is hard to turn around and go back.
Yes all things are truly possible
If only we believe
Try and find your purpose in life
The many blessings you will receive.

Open your heart and find the love
Know that you have been blessed
Remember we are all going through something
Just know this is part of the test.

FAMILY MEMORIES

Carol A. Ennis

Thank You Dad

Thank you for being the kind of dad
You taught me right from wrong,
Thank you Dad for all the man-to-man talks
It taught me to be strong.
Thank you for being the kind of Dad
You would listen when I needed to talk,
Thank you for being the kind of Dad
who took me for those long walks.

Thank you for being the kind of Dad
You showed interest in all I did,
Not only when I became a grown up
but even when I was a kid.
Thank you Dad for being a part of my life
you never tried to tell me what to do,
Even when I stumbled and fell down
you were there to help me through.

Thank you for being so understanding
when I wanted to do things my way,
When I messed up I felt really bad
you told me that it was ok.
I have so much respect for you Dad
I think you already know,
You taught me all the important values in life
that is why I love you so.

Heartfelt Expressions

Even the times when I needed a friend
you were always there for me,
If you had not been a part of my life
I don't know where I would be.
So I say to you with love in my heart
I am grateful for my life today,
You are the best Dad a son could ask for
Thank you for paving the way.

Carol A. Ennis

My Mother

My mother was someone special
She bought me into this world,
The one who cuddled and held me tight
when I was just a little girl.
My mother is the kind of person
I could call her when I was blue,
My mother was someone I could confide in
when I didn't know what to do.

My mother always listened to me
no matter what I had to say,
My mother was the kind of person
I could call her most any day.
My mother was the kind of person
she would wipe away all my tears,
My mother was the kind of person
she would take away all my fears.

My mother was so thoughtful
she had so much love to give,
Growing up without the love of my mother
would have made life so hard to live.
My mother was the kind of person
who's love can't be replaced,
My mother was the kind of person
who's memories can never be erased.

Heartfelt Expressions

My mother was kind and generous
loving in every way,
You truly would have loved her
if she were here today.

Carol A. Ennis

Two Beautiful People

What a beautiful couple
two people who became as one,
who shared in each other's joy and tears
who's lives were also full of sun.
They survived the many storms in their life
never gave up the fight,
Two people who spent their lives together
making sure that things were right.

Continuing to stay in love with each other
riding out the waves and the tide,
surviving whatever may have come their way
they did it with a lot of pride.
Though many tears and pain to bear
they still had much love to share,
two very strong willed people
is what made them such a beautiful pair.

Through thick and thin and hardships
the two were still able to stand,
all because of the vows they made
In their new life they will walk hand in hand.

Carol A. Ennis

The Love of My Sister

You are the kind of sister
So full of love and care,
Even though you didn't have much
You always seem to share.
Many times when I was feeling down
You knew just what to say,
You were always there to listen
You brighten up my day.

It's not all about just loving you
Because of the things you do,
It is because you are truly special
I realize you were just being you.
You are such a strong willed person
You let nothing stand in your way,
You are truly an amazing lady,
What more is there to say.

You took such good care of mom and dad
Which took a large part of your life to do.
They both lived a long and wholesome life
A lot of it had to do with you.
That is just the kind of person you are
Loving in every way
Your caring ways and nurturing
You give of yourself every day.

Carol A. Ennis

All of us experience hard times
You and I both know,
When one of us is in trouble
You always seem to show.
You held up a lot of forts in life
No one could tear them down,
You are a beautiful person
I love having you around.

You have the strength of a lion
A heart made of pure gold,
I hope all of your dreams come true
With the many blessing that life may hold.
I know you live your life serving Jehovah
It is He that you can always depend
I know you want to see your family again
When this old life comes to an end.

Peace At Last

We can see the golden sun rise
Now that your ship has sailed across the sea
For we know you are in a peaceful place
Now that you have been set free.

You have come to the end of life's journey
No more tears or pain to bear
Leaving behind your precious memories
For all of your family members to share.

Death cannot kill what never dies
For your love will remain in our hearts
It was so hard for us to let go
Knowing that we would be apart.

We know that we must continue on
No matter what life may hold
Your loving spirit and the image of your face
Shall never ever grow old.

You were our ray of sunshine
Even when it started to rain
We all know that without you
Our lives will never be the same.

Carol A. Ennis

I Remember

I remember when you use to play ball with me
Even though I didn't know how to play.
I remember the time I scraped my knee
You said I would be ok.
I remember the walks we took in the park
All the neat stuff we use to do
I was such a happy kid back then
I owe it all to you.

I remember the time you bought me a bike
I told you I didn't know how to ride
You gave me so much confidence
You were right there by my side.

I remember at camp I lost my gear
You drove all the way out of town
You bought more gear and gave me a hug
That is why I love having you around.

I remember the day I was late for school
I ran but I missed my bus
You got in your car and drove me to school
You didn't even put up a fuss.

I remember I was in a play at school
You were clapping oh so loud

Heartfelt Expressions

You told the teacher I was your son
You told her I made you proud.

I remember when mommy caught the flu
You cooked us something to eat
When we finished eating our food
You gave us a really good treat.

I remember you took me on your boat
We sailed across the sea
I watched the waves and the ships go by
I was happy as I could be.

I remember my first pair of roller skates
My baseball and my bat
The part I really loved the most
Is when we use to sit and chat.

Carol A. Ennis

A Mother's Love

Dear Mom,

You are a beautiful loving and thoughtful Mom,
you have so much love to give
Without you in my life Mom, life would be so hard to live.
You have always fulfilled all of my needs,
 you can always sense when something is wrong
You have always been there to comfort me,
you were there to keep me strong.
Even when something is on my mind,
I don't even have to say
You would give me words of wisdom in a very loving way.

You are always cooking my favorite foods,
especially your cakes and sweet potato pie
The love you show to your grand and great grand kids
With the beautiful gifts and clothes you buy.
I really have to tell you Mom,
your cooking is out of site
Everything is cooked to perfection,
and is always seasoned just right.

Heartfelt Expressions

One of the things I love most about you,
is that you always wear a smile
Whatever it is that I ask of you,
you would go that extra mile.
You are the kind of Mother,
so full of love and care
No matter what you may have been going through,
there was always something left to share.
It is not all about just loving you Mom,
because of all the great things you do
But because you are a good role model in our lives,
and I pray my kids grow up to be just like you.

You are a strong-willed person,
you let nothing stand in your way
You have made a difference in my life,
this I can truly say.
You are the best Mother a daughter can have
I love you for the beautiful woman that you are,
I love you the same each and every day,
whether you are near or far.
I have so much respect for you,
how you taught me the value of living
But most of all you are an important part of my life,
You taught me the gift of giving.

Carol A. Ennis

My Precious One

Rock-a-bye my baby, don't you fret or weep
Mommy is here with you, to rock you fast asleep.
Rock-a-bye my baby, don't you shed a tear
Mommy is here with you, and always will be near.
Rock-a-bye my baby, there is no need to cry
Mommy is here with you, to sing you a lullaby.

I prayed for a healthy baby,
and I thank God for this day.
When I first felt your heart beat,
it brought joy in every way
The first day I laid eyes on you,
those little tiny feet
When I held you in my arms,
your smell was oh so sweet.
You wrapped your fingers around mine,
you had a real tight grip
And then you yawned and closed your eyes,
and curled up your precious lips.

The pitter-patter of your feet
when you first learned to walk,
And when you said your first word,
when you had learned to talk.
Your eyes are like glass crystals,
they glow when it is night

Heartfelt Expressions

Just holding you my precious one
makes everything alright.

I can feel the softness of your skin,
you remind me of a dove
It was God's grace and His mercy,
for He has sent you from above.
You are my life, you are my joy,
I praise God for His giving
Because the day that you were born,
it made my life worth living.

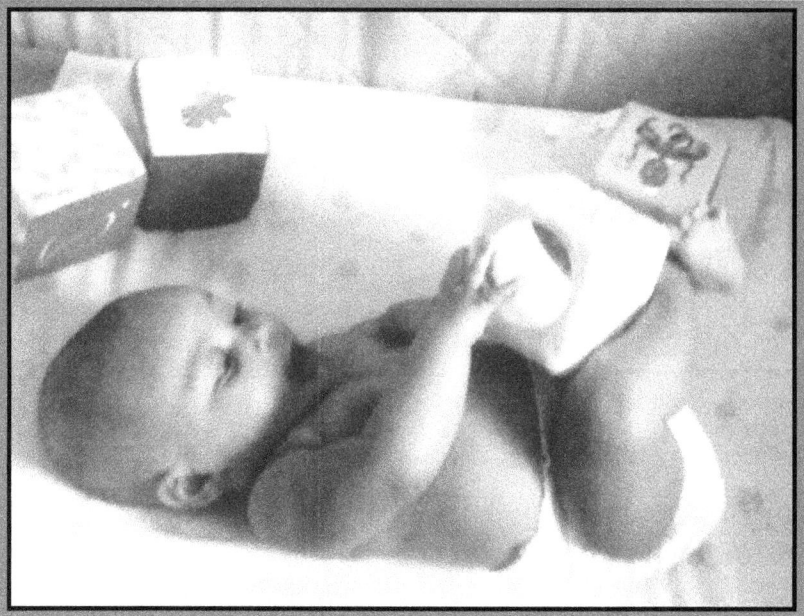

Carol A. Ennis

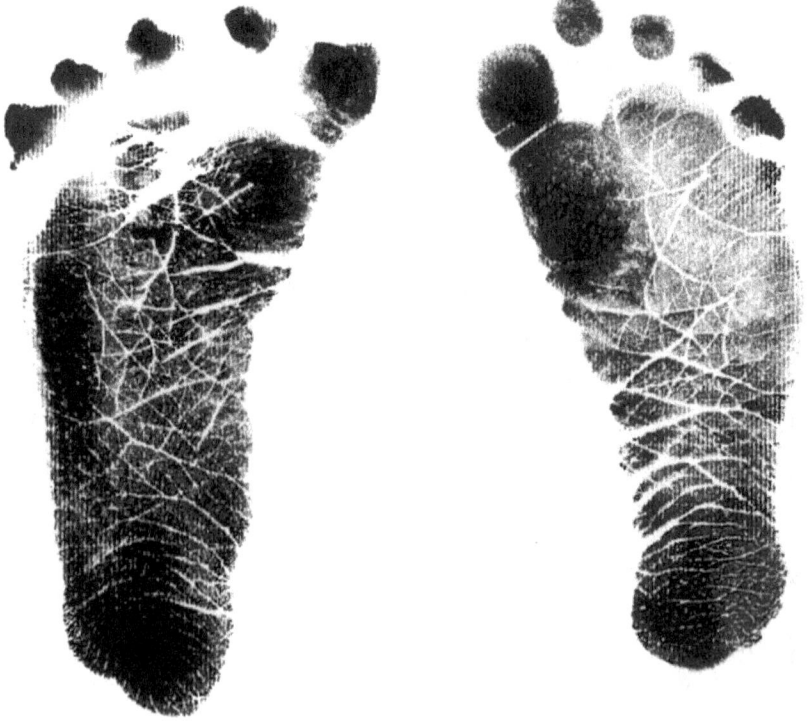

Heartfelt Expressions

Little One

A little one has come into this world
A beautiful little baby girl.
With features of her mom and dad
To hold her how it will make you glad.

To hear her cry the sound is so sweet
To watch her wiggle her tiny feet.
A gift from heaven came down to earth
A loving mom has given birth.

Your sweet and loving little one
Will brighten your lives with so much fun.
The care and love of being raised right
She will always have that glow of light.

Your baby is an expression of your true love
Cherish this gift God has sent from above.
Two beautiful parents to show her the way
You will always remember that special day.

Teach her to grow in a Christian way
To carry God's love in her heart every day.
So I say this to you both husband and wife
I pray she will add new meaning to your life.

Our Family Picnic

Mom would wake us up early in the morning
Even though it was still dark
She said we had to get started early
If we wanted to get a good spot in the park.
We loaded up the stuff in Dads Blue Station Wagon
Off to the park we went
We all busted out in laughter
In the back of Dad's head there was some lent.

We arrived at the park and started unpacking
Dad was busy lighting up the grill
We didn't have time to eat breakfast
So we couldn't wait to get that first meal.
Since it was still early in the morning
You could feel that summer breeze
There were leaves scattered all over the grass
That had fallen from the trees.

We spread the cloths on the tables
We were starving and ready to eat
We all sat down at the table
Most of us in our bare feet.
We had hotdogs, burgers, and chicken
Cases of soda and water too
We had so much food in front of us
We didn't know what to do.

We set up our blankets on the green grass
Some blankets we spread under the trees

Heartfelt Expressions

As soon as we got comfortable
Along came those pesky bees.
Now it was time to play some games
We played volleyball and hide-and-go seek
When your turn came you had to cover your eyes
But we knew some of us took a peek.

We got so excited when we saw the ice cream truck
After the ice cream truck we ran
Dad would always treat us to an ice cream cone
We always looked forward to the ice cream man.
At this type of park there were no amusement rides
There were fake horses and an old rusted merry-go-round
There were swings, monkey bars and big curly slides
If you go too fast you would hit the ground.

We always took our own music to play
We would be jamming to the sound of the beat
Then we had to take a breather
We were sweating from all of that heat.
It was time to clean up and get ready to go home
Daylight was fading and it was getting dark
When we had finished packing up all of our stuff
We loaded up and headed home from the park.

Carol A. Ennis

You Made Us Proud

All these years you struggled through school
You showed us it was not in vain
You stuck it out through thick and thin
You had everything to gain.

You made us so very proud of you
The way you handled yourself
To look at you on this special day
You are a beautiful picture of health.

Now that you have graduated
Entering a new and challenging world
Remember you will always be special to us
You will always be our little girl.

You have become quite a young lady
Just as grown up as you can be
A lot of doors will open for you
You certainly hold the key.

Success does not come easy
For you God has paved the way
Remember He is always with you
Not just tomorrow but every day.

Heartfelt Expressions

We may not have told you often enough
How much you mean to us
But we have that strong bond of love for you
In our hearts you have earned our trust.

You found a purpose in your life
It wasn't about fortune or fame
We both just want to tell you
We are proud you carry our name.

Carol A. Ennis

A Parent

A parent is one who sets up principles
To teach their children how to live
To protect them and to strengthen them
They teach them how to give.
They build a strong foundation
Teaching them to be the best they can be
Playing a dominant role in their lives
Praying they will stay drug free.

Being a good role model
They will correct them when they are wrong
Demonstrating acceptable behavior
Discipline is what makes them strong.
Taking the time to coach them
With the things they needed to learn
Rewarding them for the good things
Never rewarding them for what they did not earn.

Strengthening them when they become weak
Building them up where they are torn down
They were there whenever they were needed
They would always be around.
Teaching them to love one another
Those are the ties that bind
Picking up the broken pieces
Never leaving a loved one behind.

Heartfelt Expressions

Nurturing one another
So they won't have to struggle to survive
Trying to make a difference in this world
Especially in each other's lives.

A close knit family comes from good stock
All the right ingredients in the stew
Have compassion for one another
That's what families do.
Giving their children some sound advice
Values to carry for the rest of their lives
If they should stumble don't give up the fight
For only the strong survive.

PEACE OF MIND

Carol A. Ennis

A Peaceful Place

When I arose this morning
I thought about my life to this day
Then my mind suddenly started to wonder
For a moment this life had passed away.

I closed my eyes for a moment
My thoughts took me to a beautiful place
Where I saw blue rivers of water
In the water I could see my face.

This place was somewhat of a paradise
Filled with echoes of laughter and love
I saw a garden filled with beautiful flowers
As the sun is shining from far above.

I saw tall trees that had been planted
Birds flying high up in the sky
Even beautiful colored butterflies
White doves that had just flown by.

The grass was so green all across the fields
The smell of nature everywhere
Then my eyes had seen a vision of my mother
I could not help but to stare.

Heartfelt Expressions

Then it all started to come together
A hereafter for our love ones to share
Now I know when I cross over
I will see all my family there.

There will be a re-union with family
I will meet them face-to-face
A paradise where I will live forever
Oh what a beautiful place.

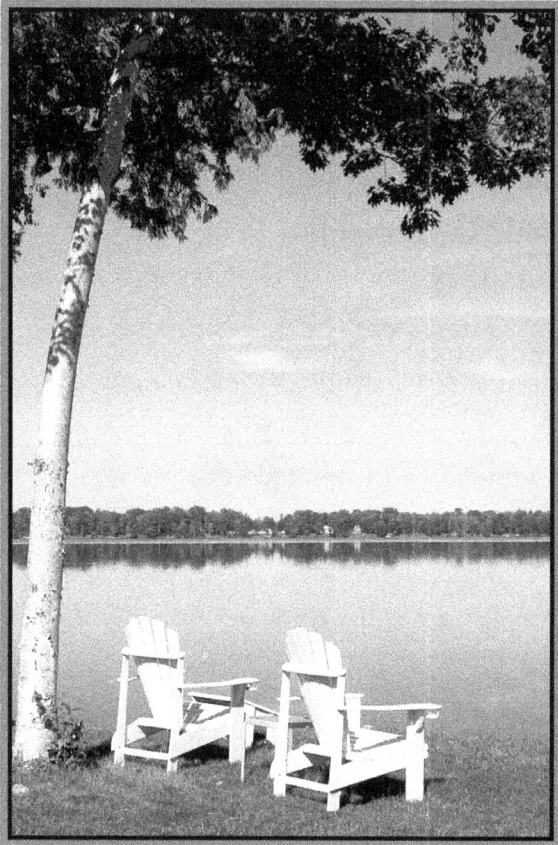

Carol A. Ennis

Deliverance

I was delivered from my darkness
When God came and set me free
He molded me into His likeness
So I can be all that I can be.
He knew I was in trouble
When He looked into my eyes
I then was delivered from bondage
That is when He broke those ties.

I felt so much shame and helplessness
There seem to be no escape
He knew about all of my struggles
He planned to put my life back in shape.
The ones I put all my trust in
Said they would be friends until the end
They were the very same people
I wind up having to befriend.

Put your faith in what you know is to be true
Let nothing stand in your way
Open your mind to all positive things
Your life will get better day by day.

Do Not Be Sad

No words could ever take the place of what you're feeling now
When you have lost a love one, you often wonder how.
It is not as if they left at once, without you ever saying good-bye
Knowing they won't be coming home, we sometimes question why.

Your love one knows you will be sad, and even shed a tear
Try to keep those precious memories alive, and the love they shared so dear.
All the pain and suffering, they will endure no more
For when they arrive at their new home there will be an open door.

You had time to prepare yourself, for what would lie ahead
You know where they are living; in spirit they are not dead.
You were blessed to have time to say some things,
You may never have said before,
Once you set your mind at peace, a knock came at the door.

You were there every minute, every wakening hour you were by their side
To give them another day of hope, even though the tears you could not hide.
They left behind so many memories, all the joyous times you had
Cherish them with all your heart, but don't let them make you sad.
So wipe away those tears of pain, and think of how it will be
For one day you will meet them in paradise
And smiles all around you will see.

Carol A. Ennis

Reborn

When you let go of the old things in your life
Your life will never be the same
That is when the light appears
You have been delivered from guilt and blame.

A heavy burden has been lifted
The many burdens you had to endure
Even some emotional turmoil
The heavy storms will be no more.

Life is full of disappointments
So many reminders of places you have been
When the evil forces come up against you
You will always win.

Take off in a different direction
But never fly with a broken wing
Put a beautiful song in your heart
So much joy a song will bring.

Take a deep breath and listen to the wind
The sweet whispers in the air
A gentle message is being sent your way
That there is nothing you cannot bear.

REACHING OUT

Carol A. Ennis

Did You

When you arose from your bed this morning
Did you plan your whole day through
Did you pray about your situation
Thank God for watching over you.

Did you ask for His forgiveness
For any wrong you may have done
Maybe you could never find the time
You were always on the run.

Did you tell someone you loved them
Maybe the words were too hard to say
Did you reach out to help the less fortunate
Or did you turn them away.

Did you give someone a hug today
Or is it always all about you
When that beggar came knocking at your door
Did you offer a blanket or some stew.
Just once if you can open your heart
Feel the pain that someone else may feel
It may change your life forever
You may have helped them to heal.

Think Before You Drink

Drinking too much alcohol can change your entire life
It can cause you to lose a lot of friends
Even lose your kids and your wife.
Most alcoholics make the statement
That they can quit at any time
But just to get that bottle
They will spend their very last dime.

Alcoholism is a sickness
There will always be a cure
Most people won't admit it
It is the pain they can't endure.
Alcohol can be dangerous
Especially when you have to drive
A lot of innocent people are dead
Who would otherwise be alive.

When you drink too much alcohol
Your thinking is not the same
So many lives are snuffed out
We have the drinker to blame.
When you have consumed too much alcohol
Your mind is not totally alert
When you cause an accident
A lot of innocent people get hurt.

Carol A. Ennis

You don't always have to drink at a party
Just to have a good time
If you are drunk and behind the wheel
You know that is a crime.
If you know you drank too much at a party
Or maybe at a night club or a bar
Be a good sport by showing you care
Give a friend the keys to your car.

When drinking set a limit for yourself
Remember you are not alone
Use common sense when drinking
The life you save may be your own.
When someone loses a love one
It is because you had too much to drink
You shouldn't have taken that drink for the road
You didn't have time to think.
It will not only affect the family
A lot of love ones it will touch
All because you didn't stop
When you knew you had too much.
It doesn't have to be hard liquor
Beer has the same affect
If you know you had enough to drink
That next drink you should reject.

Heartfelt Expressions

Think about your intake
Put yourself in the other driver's shoes.
How would you feel if you lost a loved one
Because someone drank too much booze?

Just because you drink alcohol
That doesn't make you grown
Especially when you drank too much
And wind up getting stoned.
If you know you are going to drink excessively
Choose to drink behind your own closed door
Sitting at the bar ordering drink after drink
The bartender will continue to pour.

Show someone that you love them
Don't take that extra drink
If you have to use quick judgment on the road
You will have enough time to think.
Alcohol can make you violent
Can cause you to start a fight
Always blaming someone else
Always thinking you are right.

Overcome your drinking problem
Call Alcohol Anonymous today
Take that first step in your life
There is no other way.

National Alcohol Abuse Hotline: 1-800-662-HELP (4357)

Carol A. Ennis

The LCC Gambling Fever –
Lottery/Cards/Casino

If you calculate all of those dollars you spent
Whether you add or you subtract
If you don't pick the winner
You can't get your money back.
If you go to the Casino
Play the tables or the slot machines
You will most likely walk out of the Casino
With all your pockets hanging out from your jeans.

If you double up your money
It is going to take some extra cash
You will wind up on the street my friend
Had bad luck and lost all of your stash.
You have gambled all of your money away
Now you can't even pay your bills
You will wind up in an overcrowded shelter
That is where you will be eating your meals.

When you get that gambling fever
You think you are getting hot
Then you hear those bells go off
Someone else hit your jack pot.
Every time another day goes by
You didn't win the bet
It keeps you playing anyway
Your mind has already been set.

Heartfelt Expressions

As long as the Devil is playing
You can't beat him at his game
If you go broke from gambling
You know who is to blame.
It is hard to fight temptation
You feel that you are missing out
You must change your destination
Take a different route.

Do not take sides with old Satan
He will take you for every dime
You may win a dollar here and there
But it is only a matter of time.
If you think you can't resist him
Let me give you some good advice
Stay away from the tables
Don't even roll the dice.

Which would you prefer my friend
A bed or sleeping in your car
Or trying to duck the bill collectors
Drowning your sorrows at the bar.
Maybe you haven't learned your lesson yet
You keep going back for more
Putting the hardware store out of business
Buying padlocks for your door.

Carol A. Ennis

Give up all that gambling
Put your priorities in place
Seek help for your gambling problem
The fever will disappear without a trace.
Never bet your bottom dollar
Don't even make that bid
You will never become a millionaire
Who are you trying to kid.
You always miss the number
By one digit or maybe two
If you want to kick the habit
It is totally up to you.

National Council on Problem Gambling
http://www.ncpgambling.org
24 Hour Confidential National Hotline
1-800-522-4700

A Friend From The Past

We both were friends from our childhood
Then we grew up and moved away.
We never kept in touch with each other
I still thought about her every day.

We had a good relationship
We didn't ever want it to end.
She was really a good person
She was also my best friend.

She always said she wanted to be a teacher
I told her I didn't know what I wanted to do.
The very last time we saw each other
We both said that I love you.

As the years went by I searched for her
No forwarding address that I could find.
We would always share our secrets
So many memories we left behind.

One day when I was walking
I could have sworn I had seen her face.
Then I looked again that's when our eyes had met
She started walking at a really fast pace.

I knew right then that something was wrong
I couldn't figure out why she would run away
Once I had finally caught up with her
I didn't even know what to say.

Carol A. Ennis

The first thing that came to mind to ask her
Was how are things going with you.
The tear drops began to fall from her eyes
She said I just don't know what I am going to do.

She told me she was headed for the Shelter
That is why she ran away
She was too ashamed to tell me
She didn't have a place to stay.

I placed my arms around her
She would have done the same for me
I told her my home is her home
Things will work out you will see.

She told me her life's story
How she had lost everything that she had
How fate had bought her to this town
That really made me glad.

Now she has become a teacher
She was also a friend in need
True friends are meant to be forever
From my heart I know I did a good deed.

FINDING A BETTER WAY

Carol A. Ennis

Stop The Violence

Children killing children
Gun shots ringing out in the street
Gangs hanging out on the corner
Looking for a place to meet.

People are turning a deaf ear
Afraid to report a crime
The gangs get away with the killings
They don't even serve any time.

Bad boys robbing the neighborhood
Stealing all your goods
Never reporting what you saw
Not even the witnesses would.

Running scared with weapons
Scared to leave your homes
All your windows broken out
From all of the rocks and stones.

Town Watch in the neighborhood
Trying to make things right
But every time they look around
They have to deal with another fight.

Heartfelt Expressions

Cops driving through the neighborhood
Guns cocked ready to shoot
Busting all the bad guys
Taking all of their drugs and loot.

Mothers screaming out for help
Their child gunned down in the street
Watching the ambulance take them away
All covered up with a sheet.

Guns are being sold to our children
They are scared to go to school
But if they don't protect themselves
They are teased and called a fool.

School kids being robbed each day
Their lunch money taken away
They are threatened if they tell someone
It's with their life they may have to pay.

Put your arms around your children
Tell them you love them everyday
Teach them not to use weapons
Let them know there is a better way.

Carol A. Ennis

Wake Up My People

Wake up my brothers and sisters
Keep our African culture alive
Come back to civilization
That is the only way you will survive.
Don't let the truth be hidden
Even though your enemies show their hate
Wake up from this deep sleep my friend
Or it may be too late.

Open your eyes my people
Bring the truth to the light
We must all unite closer together
We have to try and make things right.
If we continue to judge each other
By the color of our skin
We will never gain respect I say
Our hearts will never mend.

Do not be slaves to the masters
That is what they expect
They will sell you to the highest bidder
It is they who will collect.
Do not mislead your children
It is time to erase the lies
Isn't it painfully obvious
Each day a little of our culture dies.

Heartfelt Expressions

Accepting participation in corruption
Now you are engaged in physical abuse
Declare your innocence my people
Take your neck out of the noose.
Break the barriers my brothers
Wake up your Nubian Queen
Open her eyes to reality
Wake her up from this horrible dream.

Do not let her be captured
Let her not be carried away
Capture her from this world of make believe
Or oppression will lead the way.

Carol A. Ennis

The Effects of 911

After 911 our lives will never be the same
Satan was on attack that day
Trying to gain glory and fame.

But let me tell you something
Satan gets no glory here
Don't let him stop or block you
Or even put your mind in fear.

America has claimed the victory
We will put old Satan to shame
For God has all the power
He will send Satan back from where he came.

So let us come together America
Bring Satan's face to the light
Pull off all his covers
And let us be ready to fight.

May God bless our America
And for all those who lost their lives
So many love ones have perished
Men, women, children, husbands and wives.

Heartfelt Expressions

But there is a bright side that will help ease the pain
For we have not lost the fight
The rebuilding in memory of our love ones
Will turn the darkness into light.

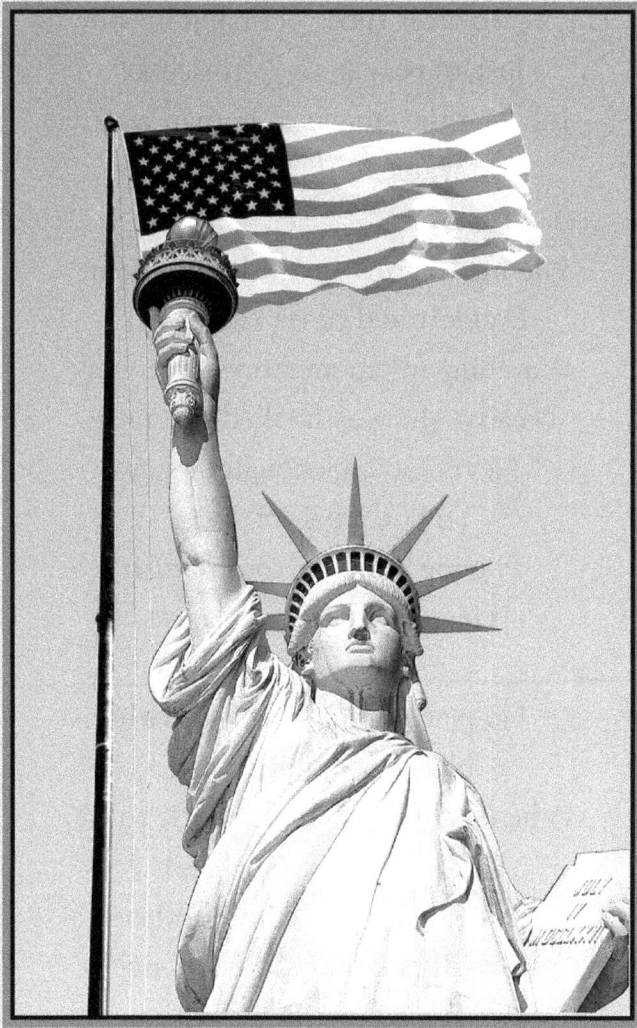

Carol A. Ennis

A Life of Poverty

Living in a world of poverty
Never having enough to eat
Sleeping in an old dirty broken down shack
No blankets, no pillows, no heat
Having to wear those old hand-me-downs
Just to be able to go to school
Inhaling the stench of human waste
No water to flush the stool.

Having to grow up with one parent
Dad left and never came back
Watching my mom stoned everyday
Because she was hooked on crack.
Never having enough money
To buy a pair of shoes
Having only one tooth brush
The one we all had to use.

No plates or folks to eat with
Not even a pot or pan
Whenever we did have a little to eat
We had to use our hands.
We do not blame our mother
She did all that she could do
When Dad was living with us
He would beat her black and blue.

Heartfelt Expressions

The thing I hate the most in life
Is selling drugs just to survive
That is the only way I knew how
To keep my sisters and brothers alive.
I know it's not right to sell drugs
About drugs in school I was taught
I only did it once a week
For fear of getting caught.

Afraid to close our eyes at night
Afraid to go to sleep
In fear of all the rodents running around
At night they would start to creep.
We couldn't afford any books for school
To keep our minds alert
How could we keep our minds on school
When living in all that dirt.

We had to live by candlelight
The only way we could see
When I tried to wake my mom up
She would start to yell at me.
Whenever she got money or food stamps
She would be gone sometimes all day
Then come home all strung out on drugs
It was the dealer she had to pay.

Carol A. Ennis

Win The Fight By Eating Right

I would like to share this message with you
There is no pleasure in being overweight
Sometimes we have the tendency
To overload our plate.
Your body is God's temple
Only the pure shall dwell within
Instead of craving for junk food
Think healthy and think thin.

We find so many excuses
For why we over eat
It is not an easy habit to kick
But it is one that you can beat.
Just add some spiritual ingredients
Like faith and praying too
Ask the Lord to guide you
Show you what to do.

While the help is on the way
You must first make up your mind
While thinking pick up an apple
Instead of that pork rind.
Eat of the fruit of the spirit
It is refreshing with every bite
Most of all it is food for the soul
It is a blessing to eat right.

Carol A. Ennis

Plan a healthy menu each day
One you can stick to
All these fast diets they never work
The choice is up to you.

Exercise and eating right is the only way to go
Ask me why I am telling you this
I lost a friend to diabetes and I know.
Breakfast lunch and dinner
Should not be all one meal
If your body continues to store all that fat
It may be your very last meal.

Take a good look in mirror
Do you really like what you see?
A mirror never tells a lie
You can be the size you always wanted to be.
Sometimes you may hear this little voice
Coming from within
Letting you know you have crossed the line
Over eating is really a sin.

No more rolls soaked in butter
All that sugar in that sweet potato pie
Fast food from the all those food chains
Eventually you are going to die.

Change your eating habits right now

Heartfelt Expressions

Set your goal to lose that weight
Refuse that second helping
Turn down that extra plate.
If you have any love for yourself
You know these words to be true
I love you my sister and my brother
Don't do it for me but for you.

Most of all you must stay strong
Now is the time to begin
Stick to the healthier choices in life
There is no way that you can't win.

Carol A. Ennis

No Place To Go

It is hard growing up in a bad neighborhood
Dealing with guns and violence every day
But my family had nowhere else to go
We were poor and were forced to stay.

Sometimes I would stare out the window
Crack vials all over the ground
Babies screaming all night long
It was such an awful sound

Cops all over the neighborhood
Blood spilled all over the streets
Gun shots ringing as the sirens sound
Bodies lying dead covered with sheets.

No smoke detectors have been installed
No fans and very little to eat
No air makes you feel so sick inside
We are already passing out from the heat.

Once you have lost everything that you had
Life will never be the same
So many families have to suffer
We wonder who is to blame.

Heartfelt Expressions

They say Hell has no fury
You'd have to be there to know how it feels
Here we are living in the ghetto
Never having enough money to pay our bills.

Must we always live in poverty?
We often ask ourselves why
The system has to make a change
Or our society will continue to die.

Carol A. Ennis

Pull the Plug and Get Rid of the Drug

There is no excuse for drug abuse
You better take heed to the word
Drugs are for the Deadheads
Or maybe you haven't heard.
Don't lead up to an addiction
Or get busted for using a drug
This is a problem we all must face
Stop sweeping it under the rug.

Drugs are bad for your body
They can do a lot of harm
Especially when you get high off of them
After sticking that needle in your arm.
Flying high is for the birds
They always land on their feet
But if you wind up getting addicted to drugs
It is a really hard habit to beat.

You started out with one small high
Enough to get you hooked
Then you found yourself getting arrested
In the line-up getting booked.
Practice saying no to drugs
Don't plant it in your head.
If you start using drugs my friend
Your brain will soon be dead.

Heartfelt Expressions

Now you can't support your habit
Or pay for your next fix
You started out just trying it
You did it just for kicks.
Now you have formed a dependency
Just to get you started on your way
You have to find a dealer
Or you can't make it through the day.

Just look at how your body shakes
Before you can get that fix
Your desperation drove your kids to the street
To support your habit they are turning tricks.
There is no limit to what you will do
To get money to buy that crack
Once your mind is too far gone
It is hard to find your way back.

You will do whatever you have to
Just to get another thrill
You will rob and steal from anyone
Or maybe even kill.
So many babies are born junkies
Because of heavy drug use
Bringing a child into the world that way
Is cruel and is drug abuse.

Carol A. Ennis

It is never the same as the very first high
No matter how much you take
Don't put those drugs in your body
Just remember your life is at stake.

Different kinds of drugs are used
They all have the same effect
If you don't learn to say no to drugs
You won't gain any respect.
So don't you be a Deadhead
Try to get back on the right track
There are resources out there to help you
Just ask they will help you get back.

National Drug Information Treatment and Referral Hotline:
800-662-HELP (4357)

HONOR

Carol A. Ennis

A Fight For Equal Rights

During Dr. Martin Luther King Jr.'s journey
He fought for what he believed was right
They took away an innocent life
Because he put up a good fight.

He lived a life of agony
Stood up for what he believed
Then he won the Noble Peace Prize
We all were quite relieved.

The Nation should try to demonstrate
All the good things he stood for
Let us join forces together
To put a stop to war.

We also should remember
His agony and his pain
So all of his accomplishments
Will not be all in vain.

He was more than just a leader of the past
He paved a way for our future to be
To teach this generation to love one another
Also how he has set us free.

Heartfelt Expressions

A man of such great courage
He had so much to give
To make this place a better world
For all of us to live.

He taught us not to judge one
By the color of the skin
He knew if we all felt that way
Neither side would win.

He stood above the balcony
Then he looked upon the sky
That is when he saw a vision
He knew that he would die.

So let us keep his dream alive
No matter how hard it may seem
To keep the promise that we made
To carry out his dream.

Carol A. Ennis

A First Lady

A highly respected and intelligent woman
Who learned to put her values first
She knows what it takes to be a first lady
Hoping for the best but prepared for the worst.
She is one to be admired, elegant in every way
She stands strong for our entire Nation
Faced with many challenges every day.

She considers everyone as being equal
Never judges by the color of their skin
If you had ever known her before
She is the same as she has always been.
It takes a lot of courage
She will always speak her mind
A down to earth and serious lady
Negativity never enters her mind.

Her life deals with the many issues at hand
Remembering where she started from
She is more than willing to take a stand
Knowing one day a change will come.
Having the responsibility of being a mother
She is also the President's wife
Her mission is to make a change
Determined to make a difference in our life.

NATURE

Carol A. Ennis

If I Were A Bird

If I were a bird I would sing and sing
And fly to the North in the early spring
So all other birds will know and can see
That I am king bird of the family.

I would flap my wings and fly so high
Until I reach the clear blue sky
If I were a bird I would find me a tree
And build me a nest for a family.

Paint Me A Pretty Picture

Paint me a pretty picture of the moon the stars and the sun
Paint me a pretty picture of the children having fun.
Paint me a pretty picture of the green grass and the trees
Paint me a pretty picture of the flowers the birds and the bees.

Paint me a picture of the rainbow; yellow, purple, blue and green
Paint me a pretty picture, one that no one has ever seen.
So when I look at this picture, Mother Nature I will see
A masterpiece for me to cherish, for you made it just for me.

Carol A. Ennis

The Lily

There is a lily in the field
that no one has ever seen
It is filled with love and tenderness
it's almost like a dream.

The lily has a wide broad steam
with buds still yet to bloom
Which makes life seem so wonderful
to grow it has much room.

That is how life appears sometimes
starting out with just a bud
Then one day the beautiful lily is gone
it was washed away by the flood.

But does this mean that all life stops
now that the lily is gone
Remember life is so precious
and life must still go on.

Just like that lily in the field
we all can one day be
If we give our love and tenderness
such a beautiful flower are we.

Where Are All The Flowers

Where have all the flowers gone
That once were planted seeds
Where have all the flowers gone
All that is left are weeds.

Where have all the flowers gone
That bloom each year in the spring
Where are all the flowers
Much happiness they bring.

The sun is beaming oh so bright
Across the fields with light
Where are all the flowers
No flowers are in sight.

A flower is so precious
One rose means I love you
So we must clear the weeds away
So we can plant a new.

Let us find the valley
Where peace we all once knew
Flowers of all colors
The grass so green once grew.

Spring Is Near

New blossoms of pastel colored flowers
Green grass is starting to grow.
Then there are the yellow honey bees
Butterflies flying low.

Squirrels are climbing up the trees
You can hear the robins sing.
When you see tulips, violets and lilacs
Then you really know it is spring.

Frogs are hopping in the pond
You can hear the laughter of children at play.
The sun is shining with a warm breeze passing
You can smell the flowers from far away.

So many beautiful spring flowers
The smell of nature is in the air.
A scene so beautiful to the eye
You can't help but to stare.

Remember this warm and sunny spring day
For the change of the season will soon be here.
When the birds, bees, flowers and trees
Have to wait until next spring to appear.

Carol A. Ennis

Days Of Summer

A clear blue sky, a summer's night
Where stars are shinning oh so bright
A new dawn brings another day
Where folks are hurrying on their way

The sound of children's laughter
While they are all at play
Families are setting up for a picnic
Even when the skies are gray

The loud noises coming from the traffic
The big tall shaded trees
The blossom of colored flowers
The sounds of the birds and bees

Never be in such a hurry
Always on the run
Life is spending time with family
Set aside time to have some fun

Listen to your heart each and every day
Families are the ties that bind
Summer time is great for family gatherings
So much joy and happiness you will find

FEELINGS OF LOVE

Carol A. Ennis

Our Love

Whenever I see a shining star
I always think of you
You always brighten up my day
I know our love is true.
Even when the sun goes down
and the darkness begins to fall
I can still see the light from my window
You are my all and all.

I can even vision your smiling face
Your hair a color of brown
I even remember your soft sweet voice
I love to hear the sound.
The perfume that you brought me
It reminds me of a flower
When I put it on my skin,
I think of you every hour.

I remember the day I touched your face
So soft and smooth was your skin
I knew I had to make you mine
It was your love I had to win.
The love we have shared together
Walking hand in hand
That is why I wed thee
With this little golden band.

Carol A. Ennis

Love Is Eternal

Love becomes eternal, the day you both say I do
A love that makes life worth living,
Lasting love your whole life through.
Love is embracing your differences
Even when things don't seem right,
Love is remembering those secret vows
The shinning of God's beautiful light.

Love is exchanging each other's love
Unlocking the key to your heart,
The joining of hands as you recite your vows
Will be the beginning of a new start.
Love is a gift that comes from the heart
God will provide you with all your needs,
For you will survive many hardships
Because you planted those mustard seeds.

Many years may come and go
Along the way there may be tears
Once your love has been rekindled again
You can look back at those memorable years.
Love demands self-surrender, a lot of sacrifices too
Love will enable you to bare the burdens
That is why God has kept both of you.

Heartfelt Expressions

Things happen in your life for a reason
Each day life presents a new change,
In keeping the promises for better or worse
Some things you may have to re-arrange.
A strong bond will keep you together
In spite of mountains so hard to climb,
The faith and the trust you believe in
Will help you leave your troubles behind.

There may be some doubts and hardships
It may be hard to walk that winding road,
At times it may seem more than you can bear
Trying to carry that heavy load.

No one in life is perfect
If we were there would be no mistakes,
You must keep the faith in what you believe
What a beautiful marriage it makes.
Enjoy your new beginning, hold up your head with pride
No matter what storms may come your way,
Stay by each other's side.

Carol A. Ennis

My Sweet Cherry Pie

I called her my sweet cherry pie
The minute I caught her eye
She glanced at me with her loving smile
Oh my sweet, sweet cherry pie.

She was a picture of beauty in every way
I could tell she was oh so sweet
It was her style and beauty that I looked upon
And I was hoping that we would meet.

Her lips were the color of a cherry
They were painted a color of red
There were feathers on her bonnet
That she wore upon her head.

She was quite an elegant lady
Her eyes were a color of blue
I stepped a little closer
To get a better view.

I walked up to this lady
I said hello my name is Stew
She spoke the words in a soft sweet voice
My name is Emily how do you do.

Heartfelt Expressions

My heart began to flutter
I could smell her sweet perfume
Her golden hair and sparkling eyes
Captured everyone in the room.

I knew I had to make her mine
Before it was too late
My sweet, sweet Emily my cherry pie
So I ask her out on a date.

Carol A. Ennis

You Are My Queen

Did I ever tell you, how much you mean to me?
I cannot think of any other place that I would rather be.
All we have shared together, all that we have been through
Nothing could ever come between us, and it is all because of you.
You are my life, you are my joy, you are my everything
I remember the day I said I do, when we exchanged our rings.

Sometimes it is an uphill battle, a lot of stormy weather
But we have become as one, and we will always be together.
Faith has kept us together, even when the sun didn't shine
We know what we have together, for I am yours and you are mine.
Nothing can ever take the place, of what is in my heart
I will always keep our love alive, nothing can tear us apart.

Life holds many treasurers, there will be ups and downs
But it comforts me to hear your voice
For I love to hear that sweet sound.
There will be some sadness, and there will be pain
Through all of our experiences we shared in life
There was always something to gain.

You are a true reflection, of how beautiful love can be
You have set a true example, and everyone can see.
I love you from the depths of my soul
You still have that loving glow
I am your King, you are my Queen
And I want the whole world to know.

Heartfelt Expressions

So I say to you the love of my life
There is nothing I would re-arrange
I love you for the beautiful woman that you are,
And I know you will never change.
Your love will forever be in my heart
I will let nothing ever tear us apart.

HOLIDAY SPIRIT

Carol A. Ennis

The Joy of The Christmas Spirit

Christmas is the time of the year
When folks are spreading holiday cheer
The smell of pine is in the air
And grandma sitting by the fire in her rocking chair.

The children sitting on Santa's knee
Presents wrapped and lay out under the Christmas tree
Shoppers are rushing to catch the sales
The sounds of Christmas carols and jingle bells.

Love ones are traveling near and far
To spend the holidays with family
So many folks are gathered around
For the lighting of the Christmas tree.

Snowflakes falling from the sky
On this cold winter night
Houses decorated with reindeers and sleighs
Oh what a beautiful sight.

What more can you wish for at Christmas time
Than spend Christmas with the ones you love
Cherish the times spent together
For it is a gift from Heaven above.

Carol A. Ennis

Hippity-Hoppity

Hippity-Hoppity goes the bunny
That means Easter is on its way
Parents are flooding the clothing stores
Buying outfits for Easter day.

Children are home dying Easter eggs
Red, blue, yellow and some green
So many different and colorful designs
The prettiest sight you have ever seen.

Easter egg hunts outside of the church
Hidden eggs were planted all around
The children with their little baskets
Filling them with the eggs they have found.

The children all dressed up in fashion
Some with ribbons and some with lace
The little girls felt so pretty
You can tell by the smile on their face.

Others had on bonnets
All shapes and different styles
Folks came to watch the Easter parade
Some traveled for many miles

Heartfelt Expressions

The little gents all dressed up in their suits
Their shoes were all shinny and new
Pastel colored shirts with bow ties
Some white and some were blue.

The children really enjoy Easter
The fun comes when they can go out to play
Un-wrap their baskets filled with goodies
They were blessed on this Easter day.

Carol A. Ennis

Be Thankful

Thanksgiving has a special purpose in our lives
Time to give thanks for all God has done
Being able to see one another again
Means the victory has been won

Thank Him for all of His blessings
For what He has done and will do
Bringing our Nation together
Their families and our families too

Thanking Him for the food on our tables
Providing a roof over our heads
Joining hands with our family and friends
Allowing us to drink wine and break bread

A time to reach out to the less fortunate
Give them hope for a better day
For we all have much to be thankful for
He allowed us to see another day

Thanking Him for all the soldiers
Who protect us while we sleep
Sacrificing their lives to keep us safe
I ask that their souls He keep

Heartfelt Expressions

If we never experienced any ups or downs
We may feel there is nothing to be thankful for
But I thank God for all things big and small
For all of His blessings and so much more

Carol A. Ennis

My Valentine

Chocolates, flowers, a teddy bear
The feeling of love is in the air
Oh won't you please say you'll be mine
My beautiful Valentine.

My heart starts to flutter when I look at you
That is how you make me feel
When I look into your beautiful blue eyes
I know the love that I feel is so real.

The joy I feel inside of me
I know that feeling will never part
In my eyes your beauty is one of a kind
You will always be number one in my heart.

Carol A. Ennis

The Little Baby Chick

It was early one Easter morning
A man was selling these baby chicks
I picked one up and held it in my hand
Boy did he start to kick.

I took him in the house to show mama
She asked where on earth did you get that chick
I said a man had a box full of these babies
She said don't you try and feed him
You don't want to make him sick.

We all had raised him from a baby
You would never believe how fast he grew
We kept him as our family pet
It was a male so we named him Cluck Cluck too.

When we hung the clothes on the line outside
Cluck Cluck would follow us all around the yard
Every step we took he would be under our feet
He made hanging the clothes very hard.

He would wake us up every morning
We would always listen for his sound
One hot summer morning there was silence
No sign of Cluck Cluck to be found.

Heartfelt Expressions

His feathers were spread all over the yard
We couldn't imagine where Cluck Cluck would go
A neighbor said someone may have stolen him
I guess we will never know.

Carol A. Ennis

Fright Night

It's Halloween my fearful friends
A cold and ghostly night
Goblins and witches flying high
Bats flying and ready to bite.

Pumpkin heads all glowing with light
Haunted castles with echoes you can hear
Unfamiliar creatures creeping in the dark
Those are the ones you better fear.

In the graveyard you can hear moaning
People walking their dogs through the park
Loud sounds of wolves howling
Then the dogs begin to bark.

Children be aware of your surroundings
When you go trick-or treating out there
Make sure you have an escort
Safety reflective strips you should wear.

Don't stop and talk to strangers
Be careful in which neighborhoods you go
If your parents can't escort you
Stick with a group of children you know.

Heartfelt Expressions

Halloween can be a lot of fun
It can also be dangerous too
Get instructions from your parents
If something happens you will know what to do.

While you are collecting your goodies
Don't get tempted to eat not one bite
Wait until you get home safely
Your parents can make sure it is alright.

So to all you trick-or-treaters out there
Keep your eyes open and be aware
There are strangers lurking all around you
It is you that they will try to scare.

About the Author

Carol A. Ennis is a Native of Philadelphia, Pennsylvania where she currently resides with her husband and nephew. Carol is a child of God, daughter, sister, cousin, wife, mother, grandmother and aunt whose family is very dear to her. Carol has always seen life in words and rhyme and at an early age began putting it down on paper. God has put words and rhyme in her spirit, her heart, her mind and her mouth. Carol is very thankful for the gift of poetry that God has given her. Her original poems are written from her own life experiences. In the fall of 1994, one of her poems was certified as a semi-finalist in the 1994 North American Open Poetry Contest. This poem was later published in the anthology *A Far Off Place*. In June 2002, some of Carol's poetry was published in the Philadelphia Tribune in Philadelphia, PA by Radio Host Nikki Taylor. Her poetry has inspired many people over the years and with her first published book of poetry *Heartfelt Expressions* she hopes to touch and inspire many more.

Email: PoetCarolEnnis@gmail.com
Website: www.carolennis.com

In memory of these special loved ones:

Nathaniel Malone, Sr. (1919-2005)

Anna L. Malone (1923-2011)

Gloria Jean Williams (1935-2011)

www.ingramcontent.com/pod-product-compliance
Lightning Source LLC
Chambersburg PA
CBHW060323070426
42446CB00049B/2007